Speaking Out on Work

An Anthology of Writing by New Writers

**Photographs by TODD BURGERMEISTER
and SUSAN SANGIOVANNI**

NEW WRITERS' VOICES
Literacy Volunteers of New York City

NEW WRITER'S VOICES ® was made possible by grants from: An anonymous foundation; The Vincent Astor Foundation; Booth Ferris Foundation; Exxon Corporation; James Money Management, Inc.; Knight Foundation; Philip Morris Companies Inc.; Scripps Howard Foundation; The House of Seagram and H.W. Wilson Foundation.

ATTENTION READERS: We would like to hear what you think about our books. Please send your comments or suggestions to:

The Editors
Literacy Volunteers of New York City
121 Avenue of the Americas
New York, NY 10013

Photo credits: "Ugly Hands" photos © Susan Sangiovanni. Photos pp. 26, 30, 34, 39, 42, 47, 51, 54, 61 © Todd Burgermeister. Photography directed by Ed Susse.

Printed in the United States of America.

97 96 95 94 93 92 91   10 9 8 7 6 5 4 3 2 1

First LVNYC Printing: March 1991

ISBN 0-929631-35-8

New Writers' Voices is a series of books published by Literacy Volunteers of New York City Inc., 121 Avenue of the Americas, New York, NY 10013. The words, "New Writers' Voices," are a trademark of Literacy Volunteers of New York City.

Cover designed by Paul Davis Studio; interior designed by Barbara Huntley.

The articles in this book were edited with the cooperation and consent of the authors. Every effort has been made to locate the copyright owners of material reproduced in this book. Omissions brought to our attention will be corrected in subsequent editions.

Executive Director, LVNYC: Eli Zal
Publishing Director, LVNYC: Nancy McCord
Managing Editor: Sarah Kirshner
Publishing Coordinator: Yvette Martinez-Gonzalez

LVNYC is an affiliate of Literacy Volunteers of America.

ACKNOWLEDGMENTS

Literacy Volunteers of New York City gratefully acknowledges the generous support of the following foundations and corporations that made the publication of WRITERS' VOICES and NEW WRITERS' VOICES possible: An anonymous foundation; the Vincent Astor Foundation; Booth Ferris Foundation; Exxon Corporation; James Money Management, Inc.; Knight Foundation; Philip Morris Companies, Inc.; Scripps Howard Foundation; The House of Seagram and H.W. Wilson Foundation.

We deeply appreciate the contributions of the following suppliers: Cam Steel Die Rule Works Inc. (steel cutting die for display); Boise Cascade Canada Ltd. (text stock); Black Dot Graphics (text typesetting); Horizon Paper Company and Manchester Paper Company (cover stock); MCUSA (display header); Delta Corrugated Container (corrugated display); J.A.C. Lithographers (cover color separations); and Offset Paperback Mfrs., Inc., A Bertelsmann Company (cover and text printing and binding).

For their guidance, support and hard work, we are indebted to the LVNYC Board of Directors' Publishing Committee: James E. Galton, Marvel Entertainment Group; Virginia Barber, Virginia Barber Literary Agency, Inc.; Doris Bass, Bantam Doubleday Dell; Jeff Brown; Jerry Butler, William Morrow & Company, Inc.; George P. Davidson, Ballantine Books; Joy M. Gannon, St. Martin's Press; Walter Kiechel, Fortune; Geraldine E. Rhoads, Diamandis Communications Inc.; Virginia Rice, Reader's Digest; Martin Singerman, News America Publishing, Inc.; James L. Stanko, James Money Management, Inc. and F. Robert Stein, Pryor, Cashman, Sherman & Flynn.

Thanks also to Joy M. Gannon and Julia Weil of St. Martin's Press for producing this book; Ann Heininger and Gary Murphy for their editorial and interviewing skills; Natalie Bowen for her thoughtful copyediting and suggestions; Helen Morris for her dedication and helpful contributions at so many stages of the book, and to Carol Fein for proofreading.

We would also like to thank the following tutors whose dedicated work with our student authors has enhanced our book: Romola Allrud, Sally Ashley, Patricia Berry, Shelly Cavalier, Bill Chirico, Marjorie Einstein, Tina Ellerbee, Nancy Erlich, Carlyn Flax, Kathleen Fogarty, Patricia Fogarty, Joann Fromkin, Jane Furse, Janet Goldberg, Lisa Gritti, Lori Gum, Elsie Gutierrez, Lynne Hale, Jennifer Hokanson, Barbara Houser,

Paula Hurley, Stella Kramer, Fred Libove, Mindy Lipsky, Nancy Love, Wendie Malick, Seth Margolis, Elizabeth McDade, Robin Power, Lisa Miller, Siu Ng, Sharon O'Connell, Margaret Parrish, Bill Piersol, Veronica Plowden, Doris Prada, Carmen Rivera, Eileen Rourke, Catherine Ruggieri, Josephine Schmidt, Deardra Shuler, Ingrid Strauch, Chuck Susswein, Liz Teasdale, Carlos Velez, Jadwiga Villa, Victoria Vought, Elizabeth Walker, Eleanore Wells, Elena Whitaker, Sarah Wilkinson, John Zaluski and Jane Zerkle. Thanks to Stephanie Butler for her research help. And to the LVNYC center directors who helped the project progress: Bruce Carmel, Pauline Clarke, Marilyn Collins, Ann Heininger, Rita Katcher, Siu Ng and Mary Ann Stevens.

For their hard work and enthusiastic participation, we would like to thank our student authors. For producing the photography for this book, we are very grateful to Ed Susse. Thanks also to Wallace Rogers and Liz of Rogers & Lerman Agency and to the models for SPEAKING OUT ON WORK: "Ugly Hands" Randy Wells, Denise Thomas; "How to Care for an Older Person" SENIOR CITIZEN: Anna M. Collins, ATTENDANT: Mary Denson, Rogers & Lerman Agency; "The Party" Robert Hampton; "The Hairdresser" Elizabeth Reiko Kubata, Rogers & Lerman Agency; "Guarding The Museum" Dwayne Langston, EXHIBIT: "The TV Set: From Receiver to Remote Control" Organized and curated by Matthew Geller. Courtesy The New Museum of Contemporary Art, New York City; "My Work" Fifi Velic; "Pants and Jeans" Rick Zieff; "Working With Children" Nilsa Moreno; "I Still Love Dancing" Angel Betancourt, Helena Sherrod; "Keep On Trying" Carmen Barclay, Rogers & Lerman Agency.

Our special thanks to those who helped us with the photography: Rita Katcher; Barbara Ingram, Director, Children's Liberation Day Care Center; Brother Gabriel, St. Mary Star of the Sea Apartments; Ray and Mario's Beauty Salon; Atlas Sporting Goods; Sue Wallman and Paul Penepento of McGraw-Hill, Inc.; Gregory Morbito Cleaning Company; Patricia Kirshner, The New Museum of Contemporary Art; and Metthe and Peter Dunk. Our thanks to Paul Davis Studio and Myrna Davis, Paul Davis, Jeanine Esposito, Alex Ginns and Frank Bergrowicz for their inspired design of the covers of these books. Thanks also to Barbara Huntley for her sensitive design of the interior of this book and to Ron Bel Bruno for his timely help.

CONTENTS

INTRODUCTION:
I WORK TO ACCOMPLISH MY DREAM
Erick Lewis

I am a bricklayer. I am a skilled worker. The work that I do is unique. It takes a lot of patience to learn to do it.

Most of the time, things seem to be going well for me. I approach my work sweet and simple, making it look easy. I never have a problem with my boss. He moves me from job to job with a smile.

I love to work hard so I can make it in life. There are a lot of things to be accomplished. The thing I want most is to build a home for me and my sweetheart and my children.

My house will be big enough to accommodate my whole family if they need a place to stay.

Building a house is my challenge in life. In my dreams, my house will be surrounded by live roses.

UGLY HANDS
Richard Washington

This is about people
with extra-large hands.
Sometimes they are called
ugly hands.
Blacksmith workers have
ugly hands.
Anyone who lifts weights has
ugly hands.
People who work on cars have
ugly hands.
Basketball players have
ugly hands.

A young man met a young lady.
From the first time he saw her,
he liked her.
But she didn't like him.
She called him
a common lower-class boy.

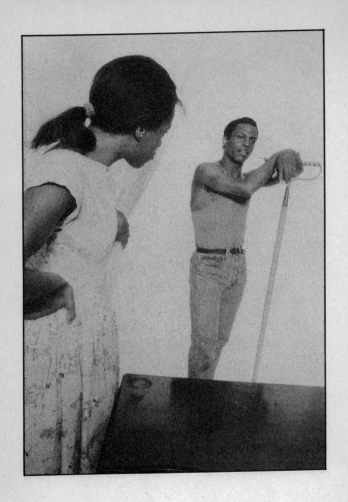

The young man had ugly hands.
The young lady called him
"the boy with ugly hands."

One day, the young man was working
in the young lady's garden.
She was getting ready
to hang new curtains.
She looked out the window
and saw him.

She just had to say something.
She shouted out,
"Get to work!"
She was so angry
just looking at him.

She climbed up a ladder
to take down the old curtains
and hang the new curtains.
But she was so angry,
she slipped
and the ladder fell.
She was left hanging.

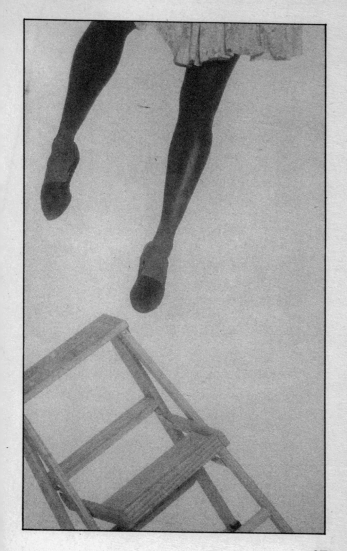

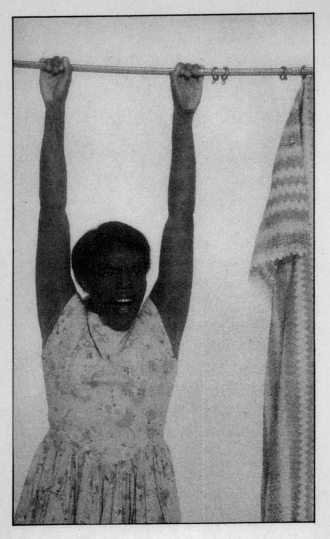

She was afraid to let go.
She called out,
"Boy! Boy!"
He didn't answer.

So she called out,
"Young man!"
And he looked up and answered,
"Yes?"

"Would you please get me
that ladder," she said.

But instead of getting the ladder,
he went right up to her.
He put his hands around her waist
and said,
"Let go. I've got you."
And he let her down very gently.

She said, "Thank you,"
and walked away.
She never looked back.

But ugly hands can do good things.

NEW YORK AND JAMAICA
Barbara Clark

I work at night. I clean up four offices and dust the desks. I go to work at 5:00 P.M. and don't get home until 12:15 A.M. I don't like it but I have to do it anyway. I am scared coming home because the train station is very lonely. I never had a job like this before.

In Jamaica, where I come from, I had my own business. I baked and sewed dresses for customers. I made my own money. I can't afford to rent a place to do this in New York. That makes it hard for me.

HOW TO SURVIVE WELDING
Gumersindo Giboyeaux

Before you begin welding, you must put on protective gear. It is important that you feel comfortable. You shouldn't rush for anything. You must concentrate on what you're doing.

You have to bring a lot of rods and you must always check your gauges. You need to have a steady hand so that you can perform your job as firmly as possible.

The better you do your job, the prouder you will be.

HOW TO CARE FOR AN OLDER PERSON
Mary Stevenson

I am a home attendant. When I get to my job, the first thing I do is give my patient a bath or shower. Then I bring her the newspaper.

While she reads the paper, I make her breakfast. After breakfast, I get her dressed. Sometimes I take her out for a walk in the park.

It's not easy taking care of an older person. But, for me, I like it.

I also take her to the doctor on the bus. Getting on and off the bus isn't easy for her. I tell her every time, "Don't worry." You have to know what to say because older people are sometimes like little children.

You have to take them in your arms sometimes and tell them you love them and you will take good care of them.

MY FIRST WORK EXPERIENCE
Patricia Bynum

The first day I went to work at the preschool, it was good. All the kids said their names and ages. We sang a song. Then we did some exercises.

During the week, I helped the kids with their homework. We played games with toys. I had them count from one to ten. We went for walks in the park.

When I went to work the next Monday, they told me I didn't have a job. Why? I never did find out the reason.

A PROBLEM AT WORK
Michael

I wanted to go on vacation the week of July 4. I asked my supervisor for the time two weeks in advance. He okayed it and said there would be no problem.

Two days later, my boss said that I couldn't go. He said he had no competent people to do my work. I told him that wasn't fair. I had made all my reservations. I was going to follow through with my plans. I said I would get someone competent to take my place. I got a buddy to agree to work the week I would be away.

I took my vacation. When I got back, my boss said I had gone without permission. I reminded him that he had okayed it. I also told him I had learned a lesson. From now on, I will put my vacation request in writing and get my boss to okay it in writing.

THE PARTY
Morris Gould

I do party work—I bartend, prepare and arrange the food, and serve. I can do anything connected with food.

I went to a lady's house to do a party. She had put out all the serving dishes. And in each dish, she put a slip of paper with the name of the food for it. I almost threw my hands up in the air because I didn't think I could read the slips.

Usually, I decide myself what food to put in each dish. But I didn't panic. For appetizers, she had lox, cream cheese, brown bread, vegetables and cheese. For dinner, she had chicken on a bed of rice, brisket, candied carrots and salad. I looked at the food and I looked at the slips of paper. And I figured out which food was for each dish.

MY BOSS
Thomas Downey

I work in a print shop. My boss and
I have worked together for 29 years.
We have become very good friends.

He helps me with my work when I
need help. When I have trouble with my
machine, he helps me fix it.

If he has a rush job, he knows I will do
it right away. He can depend on me.

We had our differences at times. When
I was wrong, I admitted it.

I am very lucky to have a very good
boss who understands me. I think he
knew that I didn't know how to read but
he never said anything about it. I told
him I was going back to school to learn
how to read. He said, "I'm very glad."

THEY BRIGHTEN UP MY DAY
Antonio Alexander

I used to be the type who waited around
thinking a job would come to me.
I circled different jobs in the Sunday
paper but never followed up.

One day, I decided to go downtown
with the paper. I wanted an easy job with
no skills required. I ended up as a line
cook in a fast-food place. Now I know all
the stations and am learning about the
chef's preparations.

Today I have a cooking skill. And I also
learned that what you want won't come
to you—you have to go get it.

I also work as a volunteer with a
program that delivers free meals to older
people. The people who are looking for
their meals are glad to see me. I am glad
to see them too. They remind me of my
grandmother. The way they greet me
brightens up my day.

THE HAIRDRESSER
Madeline

I'm learning how to read and write so I can get a better job. What I do right now is nice. You do not need to read or write at all. You just use your hands.

I'm a hairdresser. It is a great career and the money is fantastic. But when you are on your feet for 14 hours, you don't find it great or fantastic. All you know is that your feet are killing you when you go home at night. You wish that you had a nine-to-five office job.

I have to work so hard because I am a single parent. But it is very hard having trouble reading and going to school, being a mother and father at the same time, paying the bills and keeping a roof over our heads. I know going to school will pay off and I will get a good job.

THE CHEF AT LAST
Hewell Wilson

In 1977, I worked as a porter at a nutrition program. They were training me to be a kitchen helper.

I became a good kitchen helper for the first chef. My work took a lot of time and I had to stop coming to school. I was upset about that but my job came first. It was better than being on welfare.

In 1981, they promoted me to second chef. Soon after, I got a better offer from another program. I had the job for a year but I wasn't really ready for it.

So in 1982, I went back to where I had my first job. I had to start at the bottom—I was a kitchen helper again. It took me five years to work my way back to second chef.

In 1990, I wound up being the head chef. Was it worth it? Yes!

I KEEP TRYING
James

I would like to become a city bus driver.
But it is not easy. The test is hard.
I know I will have to work hard to pass
the test. If passing the test was easy,
everyone would be a bus driver. But
because it is hard, people give up.

I think that it is very wrong to give up.
I believe that if you keep on trying, you
will make it. I keep trying because I want
to make it. And when I make it, I'm going
to go out in the world and tell everyone
how good it feels.

GUARDING THE MUSEUM
Dwayne Langston

My job is in security. I protect the paintings, sculpture and video works in a museum. We usually have one of our videotapes running in the front window to attract people into the museum.

An hour into a quiet workday, a guy came into the museum yelling and cursing. He was mad about the video we were showing. "Take that damned tape out of the window," he screamed. "I don't want to listen to that crap."

I said I couldn't do anything about his complaint but I would take it to my boss. She said, "Don't worry about it. We always get weirdos in here."

If you're wondering what was on the video, I'll tell you. It was about black and white people. It said that some white people have a little bit of black in them.

I think the guy was really mad hearing this. He might be white but a long time ago, his ancestors might have been messing with blacks. I don't think he liked the idea that he could have black blood. But I think we can't be prejudiced against each other's ancestors. Peace.

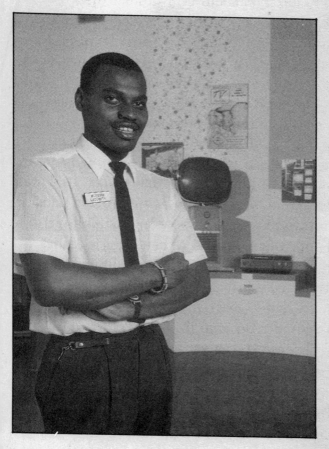

WORK AS A CHALLENGE
Catherine T.

My first job was in a bank. Before I went to work I was scared. I didn't know what to expect.

My job title was "page." I gave out the mail to all the employees.

I felt my job was the most important thing in life. When I first walked in, I was excited. Someone took me around and introduced me to people. The first girl I met was Lorraine. When I got to know her, I told her about my reading problem. She was very helpful to me.

I had to leave my job when a family member became ill. I felt very bad because it was my first job. I had learned so much. The people were great and made me feel great. I wish that I had never had to leave my job because I simply loved it.

WORKING WITH CHEMICALS
Clabon W.

I used to work in a chemical plant. One of my duties was to make pigment from raw materials. These materials were very dangerous to work with. They could be deadly if they were mishandled. We had to wear masks so we would not breathe their fumes.

One of the problems was that some of the people handling these chemicals were inexperienced. This led to many accidents.

The raw materials could be harmful to your skin. But the pigments we made from them weren't. Believe it or not, most of the pigments were used to make women's makeup.

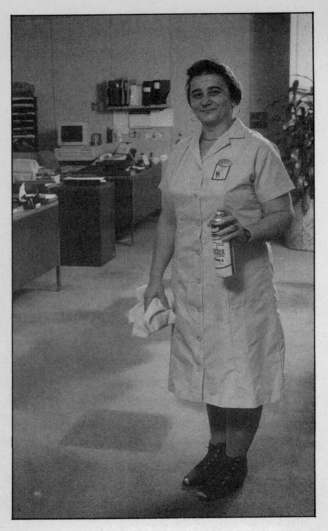

MY WORK
Martha Brown

When I was a child in South Carolina,
I had to work hard. I picked cotton in the
field. I chopped fodder and plowed. I also
served water to the field hands, planted
watermelons, stripped sugar cane and
made soap. Then I cleaned homes and
cut wood for the fires.

Now I am a custodian at a college.
It is much easier. I am responsible for
cleaning two classrooms and four offices.
I love my work.

First, I take all of the chairs out of the
room. Then I sweep the floor. If I don't
sweep the floor, it won't shine when
I wax it. I wax it in sections.

I also do eight bathrooms. I clean the
sinks. I put fresh tissue in the holders
and clean the toilet bowls.

THE BOSS DID WRONG
Joseph Phillips

I work at a restaurant as a cook.
I make dinner. I serve roast beef or
brisket with peas and carrots and gravy
with mushrooms in it. I also make
goulash with noodles and chicken
fricassee with rice.

One year, I didn't take a vacation.
At the end of the year, I asked to be paid
for the extra time I had worked. The boss
didn't want to give me my vacation pay.
I spoke up for my rights and let that boss
know that he was doing me wrong.
He gave me a hard time. So I went
to the union supervisor. He said that
I had to get two weeks' pay. Then
the boss paid me.

A PICNIC
Clinton M.

The staff of the housekeeping department at the hospital where I work had a picnic. We gave the party for ourselves because we were never invited to the parties other departments had. I was asked to set up the food for my co-workers.

After I finished eating, I was standing around talking with some of my friends. My boss called me over to ask if I knew how to cut a watermelon.

"Yassa boss, yassa boss!" I thought to myself. "Bastards like you are supposed to cut the watermelon for the workers. I have no business cutting it."

Instead I cut the watermelon.

PANTS AND JEANS
Manuel Tejeda Jr.

I work at a small department store. I used to be a salesperson for pants and jeans. After six months, they made me manager of Department 23—that's pants and jeans.

It's a very hard job because you have to know how many pants and jeans you have and you have to decide how many to order. The part I hate is counting them because we have so many.

I place my order on Thursdays. The truck brings it the next Wednesday. I have to count the new pants and jeans to make sure we got the right number.

We always have to keep an eye on the dressing rooms because some people steal.

There's one thing that makes me mad. Some customers don't ask for help finding what they want. They go through all the pants and jeans looking for the right size. They make a mess and we have to rearrange everything.

But it's a good job and I have learned a lot from it.

CATERING
Margaret W.

One day I would like to start my own catering business. The type of food I would cook is southern food. I would make pies, cakes, cookies, salads and all types of hors d'oeuvres. For example, I would serve pecan pies, hams and cheeses.

I plan to begin my business when I retire. I will move back to Charleston, South Carolina. I know I will be bored in my retirement and will need something to do. And since I like to cook, that's what I plan to do.

At first, I would run my business from my house. I would prepare the food and have others help. When the business grew, we would move to a larger place.

I know it will be very hard work at first. But I love to cook and I know I will be happy in the catering business.

THE STORE
Kenneth Torres

I work in a small grocery store. Orders
are delivered around six A.M. We take the
cases and separate them into categories.
We put each group of cases in the right
aisle. Then we pack out the boxes.

Yesterday we received 392 cases. I was
assigned to the aisle that has dog food,
baby food, flour and salt.

Every time we get a delivery, the boss
gets naggy. He gets like that because the
store is crowded. We try to let people
know ahead of time when we will get a
delivery of something they want. Then
they all come in at once to buy it. The
boss wants us to get the stuff on the
shelves as fast as possible so people
can buy it.

If everything goes well, I'll get promoted
to a bigger store that has more groceries
and aisles.

WORKING WITH CHILDREN
Nilsa Moreno

I work at a day care center as an assistant to the teacher. There are 22 children in my class. They are four- and five-year-olds. This is a crucial age because their ability to learn is so great.

I take the children to the park and watch while they are playing to see that they don't get hurt. Sometimes, the teacher asks me to ask the children what they did or saw in the park and to write it down. This is hard for me because of my reading and writing problem.
But I try my best.

We also help them see that reading and writing is fun. Sometimes I read a book to the children before they take their naps. I like this because it helps me do more reading.

I help the teacher with arts and crafts. This is good because I learn at the same time.

The people I work with are very helpful to me. When I have trouble reading and writing, they tell me not to worry about the words I do not know. This makes me feel good.

MY DREAM JOB
Anonymous

When I was a child, I did not dream of becoming a nurse's aide. But, as I got older, I realized that nursing pays well so I decided to go into it.

The first step I took was to look for a school that was registered with the state. At first, I did not know how I would make out because of my reading.

The course lasted for seven months. At the end, we had to take a final exam. It was not so hard. I passed with 89 percent. After that, I went on to get experience in a hospital.

I had always been afraid of death. I told a friend that if I was in the room when someone died, I would run out. But it did not turn out the way I planned.

A nurse was taking us around the hospital as usual. When we got to one room, she stopped and told us not to be surprised. The patient in this room was very sick. The doctor had to connect him to a lot of machines. It was a shock to me to see him. Just the day before, he had appeared healthy.

The nurse assigned me to the other patient in the room. I started to feed him. But I was looking at the patient with the fever. I was afraid of what was going to happen to him.

I kept on feeding the other patient until the nurse came in. She looked at the patient on the machines and knew something had happened. She called a code and all the doctors came running into the room.

I could not move. I was trapped on the other side of the room and could not get by all the doctors and nurses. I had to stay in the room. The doctors tried to revive him but it was no use. In 20 minutes, it was all over and the doctors left.

That was my first experience. I could not run away. Although I did not go near, I had to face my fear.

In spite of having to deal with death, this is my dream job.

I STILL LOVE DANCING
José Vila

I always wanted to be a flamenco dancer. Even as a small boy in Spain, if I heard music, I would dance to it.

One day my father said to my mother, "Let's send José and Margot" (that's my sister) "to take flamenco lessons." We started taking classes when I was seven and Margot was five.

As we got older, we danced at clubs and schools. Later we danced on television and at the World's Fair. Finally we danced with big companies like the José Greco Company. Usually we danced as a team.

As we got older, I realized that you don't make a lot of money if you don't own your own company. So we stopped and found ways to make a living outside the dance world.

But I still love dancing with all my heart.

STUPID
Anonymous

Why do people think you are stupid
if you make a mistake? They make
mistakes themselves. But they think they
know everything.

Bosses make people look stupid. All
they know is yelling and screaming at
their workers. But that accomplishes
nothing. They make themselves look
stupid with their yelling and screaming.

My bosses think they own me.
Little do they know, I have sent in an
application for another job. I am waiting
for a reply.

NANNY
G. Fraser

I have been working with Mrs. Brown for
three years. She is a very nice lady. I take
care of her son and her apartment. We
are on the 14th floor. It is in a good part
of town. I live in and go home on the
weekend.

My job is hard but I like it very much.
I have to do a lot of walking. I make up
the grocery lists and do the laundry for
the whole family.

At Christmas, my boss invites her whole
family over for dinner. They exchange
gifts. I have a lot of cleaning up
to do afterward.

I used to work with a lady taking care
of her two children. She was not nice to
me and her children weren't nice to me
either. So I left that job and got this one.

MY BOYS
Cynthia B.

I work for two men whom I call "my boys." I work for them on Monday, the worst day of the week. And every week, it's the same story.

I walk into work and there are notes all over the apartment—and I can't read them. I start to sweat and get very nervous. But I start doing the laundry and wait for one of the boys to wake up.

K. finally comes in the kitchen and says, "Good morning, Cynthia." I say, "Don't talk to me. I'm having a bad day." Then we talk about our weekends. He says, "B. left you some notes." And I say, "Doesn't he have anything else to do?"

I put all the notes together on the kitchen cupboard. K. picks them up and looks through them. "It's not so bad," he says. Sometimes a note will say something like "I want everything fire bright." And I say, "You want me to light a match?"

Have you seen the TV show *The Odd Couple?* The boys are just like Felix.

Sometimes I feel like walking out. Sometimes I feel like their mother. Maybe that is why I call them "my boys." I don't know if I could tell the boys that I don't know how to read. Maybe someday I will be so proud of myself, I will tell the world.

KEEP ON TRYING
Anonymous

I thank God for all my blessings and the job I have.

I started out as a temporary worker for the Civil Service. I worked myself up to an office associate. It wasn't easy. I had to take tests each step of the way to get promoted.

I took Saturday classes to prepare for the tests. My family helped me too. I did not pass the test the first time around. I was disappointed but I went back to my books and studied some more. The next time I passed the test. I was very proud of myself.

Recently, a woman from the Equal Employment Opportunity Commission came to talk to us about our rights. I learned a lot and some things won't happen again.

The main thing I've taught myself is not to give up on things. If you don't pass a test or don't get the promotion you want, keep on trying.

TO OUR READERS

The poems and stories in this anthology were all written by students in the Literacy Volunteers of New York City program. We hope to publish more anthologies like this one. But to do that, we need writing by you, our readers.

If you have a piece of writing you would like us to consider for a future book, please send it to us. It can be on any subject; it can be a true story, fiction or poetry. We can't promise that we will publish your story but we will give it serious consideration. We will let you know what our decision is.

Please do not send us your original manuscript. Instead, make a copy of it and send that to us, because we can't promise that we will be able to return it to you.

If you send us your writing, we will assume you are willing for us to publish it. If we decide to accept it, we will send you a letter requesting your permission. So please be sure to include your name, address and phone number on the copy you send us.

We look forward to seeing your writing.

The Editors
Literacy Volunteers
of New York City
121 Sixth Avenue
New York, NY 10013

NEW WRITERS' VOICES

A SERIES OF BOOKS BY ADULT NEW WRITERS

Calvin Miles, WHEN DREAMS CAME TRUE, $3.50

Mamie Moore, MAKE WAY FOR AUGUST, $3.50

Theresa Sanservino, CAN'T WAIT FOR
    SUMMER, $3.50

FROM MY IMAGINATION, An Anthology, $3.50

SPEAKING FROM THE HEART, An Anthology, $3.50

SPEAKING OUT ON HEALTH, An Anthology, $3.50

SPEAKING OUT ON HOME AND FAMILY, An
    Anthology, $3.50

SPEAKING OUT ON WORK, An Anthology, $3.50

TAKING CHARGE OF MY LIFE, An Anthology, $3.50

To order, please send your check to Publishing Program, Literacy Volunteers of New York City, 121 Avenue of the Americas, New York, NY 10013. Please add $2.00 per order and .50 per book to cover postage and handling. NY and NJ residents, add appropriate sales tax. Prices subject to change without notice.